PETRIFYING POEMS

Compiled by Jane Covernton
Drawings by Craig Smith

Hippo Books
Scholastic Publications Limited
London

Scholastic Publications Ltd.,
10 Earlham Street, London WC2H 9RX, UK

Scholastic Inc.,
730 Broadway, New York, NY 10003, USA

Scholastic Tab Publications Ltd.,
123 Newkirk Road, Richmond Hill,
Ontario L4C 3G5, Canada

Ashton Scholastic Pty. Ltd.,
P O Box 579, Gosford, New South Wales,
Australia

Ashton Scholastic Ltd.,
165 Marua Road, Panmure, Auckland 6,
New Zealand

First published by Omnibus Books, Australia, 1986

Published in the UK by
Scholastic Publications Ltd., 1988

ISBN 0 590 70941 0

Contents

Acknowledgements

The editor and publishers wish to thank the following for permission to use copyright material:

David Bateson for *Night Mare*; Janeen Brian for *The Ghost of Uncle Bill*, *Hairy Scary* and *Samuel Junior Spook Esquire*; Ann Coleridge for *The Cane Mutiny*, *Ravening Horde* and *You've met your match*; Michael Dugan for *Witch direction*; Sally Farrell Odgers for *Kedge*, *Witchwater* and *Catseye*; Max Fatchen for *Creaks and groans and rattling chains*, *And s-s-so to b-b-bed*, *Ghostly Gilbert found it daunting*, *That's the Spirit!* and *The vampire said: "My name is mud"*; Jeff Guess for *The Wood-Pile Shed*; Phyllis Harry for *The Groplejum*; Wilbur G. Howcroft for *To Bury the Body*; Robin Klein for *Full Moon*, first published in *Snakes and Ladders* by Robin Klein, J. M. Dent Pty Ltd 1985; Verity Laughton for *Come to Me*; Doug MacLeod for *The Viper*, *Fisher's Body*, *The Cod*, *The Bunyips*, *Attack of the Crayfish From Mars*, *Witches* and *Epilogue*; Stephanie McCarthy for *Gala Night*; Peter Wesley-Smith for *Foreword*, *Things That Go Squark*, *Dominique*, *The Loof*, *The Curse of Auntie Beth* and *Epitaph*.

While every effort has been made to trace and acknowledge copyright, for some work this has proved impossible. Should any infringement of copyright have occurred, the publishers tender their apologies.

Foreword

Marble-browed and gravel-voiced,
stony-faced and flinty-eyed:

I saw this book,
my blood ran cold;
I sneaked a look—
I petrified . . .

Dear reader, pause a while, beware—
and read on only if you dare . . .

Peter Wesley-Smith

Creaks and groans and rattling chains,
Monsters that will blow your brains,
Shudders, shakes, the nightmare scream
Come from cakes with too much cream.

Max Fatchen

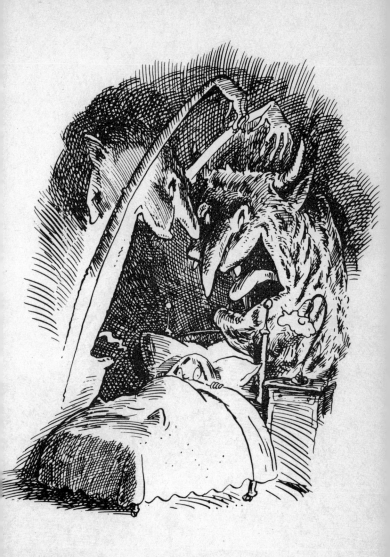

Kedge

Tracey Bone—you hurry home
You're late—it's after half-past eight
And in the park when it is dark
Old Kedge the park witch waits

As you pass along the path
Listen for her tread
If you hear it—better fear it
Listen then with dread . . .

Kedge comes sneaking, softly creeping
Shadow spiky as a tree
Steeple hat and cloak of bats
Her cackles crack with evil glee

Kedge is really weirdly bearded
Sporting warts on every chin
She waits behind the creaking gate
And rides a fitful evening wind

Kedge has twitchy, witchy fingers
Out to clutch your shrinking back
A broom to bear you to her lair
Packed inside a blackened sack—

What will happen when she's got you
Penned inside her dirty den?
Tremble then, for Kedge's victims
Are never *ever* met again!

Better race you silly Tracey
Better run behind the light
Or I betcha Kedge will getcha
As you're going home tonight!

Sally Farrell Odgers

Night Scene

out there where
the laurel hedge stood
there is a black wall
hiding in its
whispering buttresses
a blind panther
and a mad monk crouching
and a terror that
will take shape
the moment
you turn around

the fingered form
you see edging around
the corner of the tool shed
is dracula
frankenstein
the witch of endor

and a couple of werewolves
are talking in whispers
at the front gate

and every unexplored corner
of the dark
conceals a gibbering thing
not yet born
but lying in readiness
for the scream
of a horrible nightbird
that lives normally
in a sepulchre

when it screams
a thousand demons
will spring into awful life
wet winged
immense and pitiless
and batter the black air
with silent ferocity

the thing you see
over there to the right
in the pergola
is the ghost
of jack the ripper

this is what I say to
Morris Carmody
Morris is a little
thin nervous boy
he has been playing with me
tonight
as mother and father
are at the pictures
and he has to go home
by himself

Redmond Phillips

14

In a Dark Wood

In a dark, dark wood there was
    a dark, dark house,
And in that dark, dark house there was
    a dark, dark room,
And in that dark, dark room there was
    a dark, dark cupboard,
And in that dark, dark cupboard there was
    a dark, dark shelf,
And on that dark, dark shelf there was
    a dark, dark box,
And in that dark, dark box there was . . .

Things That Go Squark

There are things that go squark in the day-time,
there are things that go garkling at dawn;
there are things that gruffoon
in the late afternoon
or whenever the curtains are drawn.
There are things that go swoosh in the morning,
there are things that enfooble and fight;
ev'ry ev'ning at dusk
there are things quite grotusque,
there are things that go bump in the night.
There are things that go squelch in the spring-time,
there are things that go flark in the fall—
but the worst of the breed
is a terror indeed:
it's a thing that goes nothing at all!

Peter Wesley-Smith

And s-s-so to b-b-bed

"Do go to bed," they're saying
But do they know what's there,
Within that crowded darkness
Or shrieking through the air?

What's that upon the bedrail?
What's hiding underneath?
There could be miles of crocodiles
With big, expectant teeth.

"Now go to bed this instant!"
But have they ever dared
The shadows in the passageway?
Were parents *never* scared?

"Now into bed." Their voices—
Are rising to a shout.
But when they turn the light off

It's then the THINGS come out!

Max Fatchen

The Wood-Pile Shed

When the fire burns low on a winter's night
and the wood-bin holds not a stick
and Dad's been asking for over an hour
but the night is as cold as it's thick.

Your mouth is dry and your legs won't move
and you tremble with fear at the thought
of the long slate path without a match
all alone without help or support.

You've been before in the depths of July
when the wind and rain sweep in
with a rusty barrow to the back of the yard
through a night that's as black as sin.

You know what waits in cold dark earth
though its face you never have seen
the scream, and scuttle and shadow that moves
in the thin brief silver moon-beams.

O eyes that shine in the wood-pile shed
and the thousands of legs beside
that scratch and scramble and bump and tap
where there's no warm blankets to hide.

Things that touch and things that creep
and you'd run like mad if you could
from all the horrible things that wait
in the stacked cut mallee and wood.

There's nothing as cruel on a winter night
and nothing that equals the dread
of a father who doesn't understand
your fear of the wood-pile shed.

Jeff Guess

The Groplejum

In the cellar there's a sound
Like something nasty moving round.
"The wind," Dad says. "The cat," says Mum.
But *I* know it's the Groplejum.

The Groplejum sleeps in the day
But when it's dark he starts to stray,
Seeking what I do not know.
I wish he'd go. I wish he'd go.
He's terrible. He snarls. He roars.
One foot has toes, the other claws.
And oh, the horror of his eyes!
They're licorice-black and big as pies.
His mouth's a cave. His awful tongue
Is cheesy blue, a metre long,
And when he breathes the air round glows
With flames that rush out through his nose.

When it's sunny, when it's bright,
I enjoy the Grople, quite.
I add a detail here and there
Like meat-hook hands and orange hair.
But come the night, I always feel
This prowling monster's real as real.
And then I'm sorry I invented
The Groplejum, however splendid.

Phyllis Harry

Night Mare

The Night Mare gallops past our house;
    the neighbour's clock chimes ten;
    she gallops past the cemetery,
    and wakes up buried men.
I'm left here in the house alone,
    while Mum works at the club;
    my sister's at the blue-light dance,
    and Dad's still at the pub.
I hear the hooves on cobblestones,
    though our street's sealed with tar;
    I hear her clumping through wet grass,
    although the fields are far.
No other person hears this mare,
    just me when I'm in bed,
    but though she scares me in my dreams
    I wouldn't wish her dead.
One night I'll put away my fears
    and wait for her outside;
    I'll jump right up on to her back
    and take her for a ride.
Our moonlight race will frighten thugs,
    or murderers who prowl;
    we'll scare the burglars in dark lanes,
    and hush the ghosts that howl.

David Bateson

The Ghosts' High Noon

When the night wind howls in the chimney cowls,
    and the bat in the moonlight flies,
And inky clouds, like funeral shrouds, sail over the
    midnight skies—
When the footpads quail at the night-bird's wail,
    and black dogs bay at the moon,
Then is the spectres' holiday—then is the ghosts'
    high noon!

As the sob of the breeze sweeps over the trees, and
    the mists lie low on the fen,
From grey tombstones are gathered the bones that
    once were women and men,
And away they go, with a mop and a mow, to the
    revel that ends too soon,
For cockcrow limits our holiday—the dead of the
    night's high noon!

And then each ghost with his ladye-toast to their
    churchyard beds take flight,
With a kiss, perhaps, on her lantern chaps, and a
    grisly grim "good night";
Till the welcome knell of the midnight bell rings
    forth its jolliest tune,
And ushers our next high holiday—the dead of the
    night's high noon!

W. S. Gilbert

28

The Viper

Inside the Lighthouse Jellybone
Old Jim the keeper sat alone
The waves were high, the stars were dim
And spirits seemed to call to him,
"Be sure to watch the Jellybone light
Or sailors' ghosts will rise tonight!"

And then a voice cried, "Keeper Jim!
I am the *viper*, let me in!
I'd gladly serve you evermore
If only you'd unlock this door!"

Now Keeper Jim was brave and bold
But that strange voice had turned him cold
"Please go away from here!" he stammered
And still the *viper* bashed and hammered,
"I am the *viper*, let me through
For I've a special job to do
I'd gladly serve you evermore
If only you'd unlock this door!"

Jim closed his eyes, he prayed, he cried,
"Oh save me from that thing outside!"
The thunder rolled, the lightning flashed
And still the *viper* hammered and bashed
The door collapsed in all the din
And then a stranger wandered in . . .

"I am the *viper*," the stranger piped,
"Do you *vant* your *vindows viped*?"

Doug MacLeod

Ghostly Gilbert found it daunting
When his mother sent him haunting.
"What," he shrieked, "is that I'm seeing?"
It was just a human being!

Max Fatchen

Witch Direction

Wanda the witch
could never tell which
was her left and which was her right.
This troubled her when
one evening at ten
she mounted her broomstick for flight.
She set off to fly
across the dark sky
on a visit to north Transylvania,
but found to her shame
when morning light came,
she had landed in southern Tasmania.

Michael Dugan

Dominique

I heard a shriek
from Dominique
her eyes are wide
she's terrified
I don't know why
she made that cry
there's nothing there
to cause a scare
she's very weak
is Domin—EEEK!

Peter Wesley-Smith

Full Moon

At times of full moon—
I wish I knew why—
I get this strange yearning
to howl at the sky!

For reasons peculiar
I've not yet discovered,
the backs of my hands then
with fur become covered!

My fingernails lengthen,
my hands look like . . . paws!
I feel a compulsion
to walk on all fours!

My eyes redly glimmer,
hair sprouts from my ears,
fang-like my teeth grow,
with points sharp as spears!

Though normally fussy
about what I eat—
on nights when the moon's full
I crave RAW RED MEAT!

Robin Klein

The Ghost of Uncle Bill

The unwinking eye of the full-blown moon
Rose high past the mountain sill.
It cast its gaze on a graveyard cold
And the ghost of Uncle Bill.

The bride he'd married ten summers ago,
Coal-black her eyes and hair,
Moved like a cat on a prowl-tread night,
A wolf, on guard its lair.

Bill saw his bride through eyes of love,
Saw nought that was not fine.
He did not see the evil glint,
Nor hear the wolf-like whine.

The days they passed and villagers talked,
They feared the dark-eyed bride.
She moved among them silently,
And hushed, they moved aside.

Bill heard their dark-mouthed whisperings,
In anger, called them foul.
But fear gripped Bill, one moonlit night,
When he heard her wolf-like howl.

The villagers talked of voices heard,
Raised loud in the blood-chill night.
They talked of clouds that smothered the moon
Made dark her rounded light.

The moors were black when the scream rang out
Down by the muddy mill.
Now shines the moon on a graveyard cold,
And the ghost of Uncle Bill.

Janeen Brian

Witchwater

Glimmering, shimmering down by the clearing
Under a shadowing tree
Witchwater's waiting to catch the uncaring
And nobody knows it but me
Green in the evening and blue afternoons—
Silvery under the stars
Witchwater's beautiful, glowing and beckoning
Calling with dangerous charm

Enchanted and dreaming I'm here in the clearing
I wait by the shadowing tree
Centuries pass since I looked in the water
But time doesn't matter to me
Whoever you are and whatever you're seeking
Hurry away and be free
Don't look in the water—the fathomless water
Or you'll be a statue like me!

Sally Farrell Odgers

Come to Me

Come to me my little dearie,
Come to me my little child:
Do not sleep but lift your weary
Head and hark to me a while.

Look, my lovely, look, my treasure,
See, your granny's eyes grow dim.
This, dear, is no human pleasure—
Hold my hand, I'll take you in.

Can you see them, coldly waiting?
Drift and chill of breath and bone?
Dear, they move like silence skating
Past an icy, shivered moan.

Ah, my love, their red eyes brighten,
See, they like your sweet red cheeks . . .
They seem, you say, rather hungry?
Treasure, they've been starved for weeks!

Now they drift like smoke towards you,
Now they fasten to your skin.
Child, your manners, I should warn you,
No complaints when the teeth go in!

There now, it was all quite simple,
Over now, my deathless dear.
Sweet, your cheeks acquired a dimple,
Those fangs, now, what a charming sneer!

Verity Laughton

Catseye

"Watch," said the witch unto her cat
"Watch and wait till I be back.
I be going down the hill
Folk have need of witch's skill."

Catseye, catseye, green as glass
Tens of scores of years do pass

The cat sat down with folded paws
The cat sat down and watched the door
Sunrise came—the witch did not
The fire went out beneath the pot.

Catseye, catseye, green as glass
Tens of scores of years do pass

Daylight faded, daylight died
Sunset flared across the sky
Stars and moon uncaring came
Cat with watchful eyes remained

Catseye, catseye, green as glass
Tens of scores of years do pass

A plague had come and struck and killed
Since the witch went down the hill
The village crumbled, turned to grass
Tens of scores of years did pass

Catseye, catseye, green as glass
Tens of scores of years do pass

Trees grow tall across the way
That once led to the witch's cave
But—"Watch," said the witch unto her cat
"Watch and wait till I be back."

Catseye, catseye, green as glass
Tens of scores of years do pass

So sleepless, ageless, waits the cat
For his mistress to come back
Summer sun dissolves in rain—
He watches till she comes again

Catseye, catseye, green as glass
Tens of scores of years do pass

When will Catseye vigil end?
Reunited with his friend?
When the earth grows tired and still—
Perhaps—
       the witch will climb the hill.

Catseye, catseye, green as glass
Tens of scores of years have passed.

Sally Farrell Odgers

To Bury the Body

Oh, bury the body down deep in the woods,
   In a beautiful hole in the ground,
   Where the halipods howl
   And the pongaloids prowl
While the gallipods gallop around,
                  Ha, ha!
   The gallipods gallop around.

Oh, bury it deep 'neath the roots of a tree,
   Where the diddle-dits dither and dance,
   Where the beetle-bubs brawl
   And the bumble bees bawl
As the pollywogs pivot and prance,
                  He, he!
   The pollywogs pivot and prance.

Oh, dig the grave deftly and dig the grave deep,
   Whale away with the mattock and pick
   So the guillotine gorse
   Can grow compact and coarse
And the poison plant pleasingly thick,
                  Ho, ho!
   The poison plant pleasingly thick.

Wilbur G. Howcroft

Fisher's Body

From the marsh beside the creek
Fisher's body rose,
Leeches on its fingertips,
Mud between its toes.

Through the streets of Campbelltown
Fisher's body came,
Looking for a gentleman,
Worral was his name.

Through the door, up the stairs
Fisher's body crept,
Sat itself upon the bed,
In it, Worral slept.

Tossing, turning, whimpering,
In the moonlight dull,
Worral woke to see the pits
Of Fisher's grinning skull.

To the court of Campbelltown
Worral told his tale,
He was Fisher's murderer,
Justice did prevail.

In the marsh beside the creek
Where the ghost gums grow
Worral's body hangs above,
Fisher's sleeps below.

Doug MacLeod

51

There's Only Two of us Here

I camped one night in an empty hut on the side of a
    lonely hill;
I didn't go much on empty huts, but the night was
    awful chill.
So I boiled me billy and had me tea, and seen that
    the door was shut,
Then I went to bed in an empty bunk by the side of
    the old slab hut.

It must have been about twelve o'clock—I was
    feeling cosy and warm—
When at the foot of me bunk I sees a horrible
    ghostly form.
It seemed in shape to be half an ape with a head like
    a chimpanzee,
But wot the 'ell was it doin' there, and wot did it
    want with me?

You may say if you please that I had DTs or call me
    a crimson liar,
But I wish you had seen it as plain as me with its
    eyes like coals of fire!
Then it gave a moan and a horrible groan that
    curdled me blood with fear,
And, "There's only two of us here," it ses. "There's
    only two of us here!"

I kept one eye on the old hut door and one on the
    awful brute;
I only wanted to dress meself and get to the door
    and scoot.
But I couldn't find where I'd left me boots so I
    hadn't a chance to clear;
And, "There's only two of us here," it moans.
    "There's only two of us here!"

I hadn't a thing to defend meself, not even a stick
    or stone;
And, "There's only two of us here!" it ses again
    with a horrible groan.
I thought I'd better make some reply, though I
    reckoned me end was near:
"By the holy smoke, when I finds me boots there'll
    be only one of us here!"

I gets me hands on me number tens and out
    through the door I scoots,
And I lit the whole of the hillside up with the sparks
    from me blucher boots.
So I've never slept in a hut since then, and I tremble
    and shake with fear
When I think of that horrible form wot moaned,
    "There's only two of us here!"

Edward Harrington

The Sprinting Shearer

He was a gunshearer, a ringer of sheds who had
    come to the end of his run,
He let out a yell and threw down his blades when
    the last of his pen was done.
Then he went to the office and asked for his
    cheque, the Manager paid him in cash.
He rolled his blankets and started for home ere he
    gambled at cards and got rash.

He camped for the night in some trees by the road,
    away from the cold and the damp,
When a swagman came out of the evening dusk and
    started to make his camp.
"Come and join me, old-timer," the shearer said,
    "I've got enough tucker for two."
"Well, me tuckerbag's light," the old fellow said.
    "Thanks, mate. I don't mind if I do."

When the meal was over they started to talk the
    way that travellers do,
The old man said, "You been travelling long? Your
    swag and your blankets look new."
"No. I'm not on the track," the shearer said. "I'm a
    shearer just finished me run;
And I've five hundred dollars in this here purse to
    prove that me job's been done."

"Oh? Five hundred dollars?" the old man said.
"That's a lot of money, me son.
There's many a man been murdered for less and
buried some place on the run."
Then he went to his bag and took out a knife and
also a sharpening stone.
As he sharpened the edge he looked up and said,
"You should never have travelled alone!"

The shearer thought what a fool he'd been to open
    his mouth so wide,
He was sure the old man would wait till he slept
    then bury the knife in his side.
So he lay in his blankets and waited to hear the
    sound that the swagman slept,
When he heard the first snore he slipped out of bed
    and into the darkness he crept.

He hadn't gone far when he thought he could hear
    footsteps not far at his back,
So he quickened his pace from a walk to a trot, but
    those feet kept pounding the track.
At last he was running flat out in the dark, with fear
    he was almost blind,
But the faster he went, the faster they came, those
    footsteps pounding behind.

Then he stumbled and fell with a terrible thud over
a log on the track;
As he lay there gasping he fancied he felt the point
of the knife in his back.
There he trembled with energy spent, he knew that
his race had been run,
When the swagman fell over the log at his side and
whispered, "Who's after us, son?"

The shearer heaved a great sigh of relief and said,
"No one's after us, Dad!"
"Well, if no one's after us," the swagman said,
"what the hell are we running for lad?"

Mac Cormack

The Cod

At Tocumwal, the Murray cods
Play tug-of-war with fishing rods
Hence fishermen from year to year
Mysteriously disappear.

The biggest, meanest cod of all
Resides at sleepy Tocumwal
And boasts about his score to date
It's humans: nil, codfish: eight.

In order to amend this score
A ghastly girl called Eleanor
In search of bigger fish to fry
Resolved to land it high and dry.

She fished with flies and fancy hooks,
A dinghy and some fishing books,
Till late that night the codfish struck
And tipped her deftly in the muck.

She struggled to the riverside
"All's fair in love and war!" she cried
And added, tossing in a bomb,
"There's plenty more where *that* came from!"

The bomb went splash and down it sank
The codfish leapt towards the bank
Declared "All's fair in love and war!"
And spat the bomb at Eleanor.

As shockwaves rocked the river shelf
The codfish pondered to himself
"Till next they match their wits with mine
It's humans: nil, codfish: nine."

Doug MacLeod

Hairy Scary

"Oh!" shrieked the barber, in wild alarm,
As through the door came a hairy arm.
The body followed, twelve foot high,
With eyes as black as a stormy sky.

The barber shrank from the towering ghoul
Who stank of slime from a steamy pool.
His thick black hair, alive with fleas,
Hung down like rope, way past his knees.

"What do you want?" cried the barber, wild-eyed,
The monster turned and pushed him aside.
His head creased up in a terrible frown,
"A haircut," he said. And sat himself down.

Janeen Brian

The Bunyips

At Murray Bridge the bunyips wait
For visitors from interstate
Then up they leap, a sight so strange
And always out of camera range.

The tourists in their mad despair
Start seeing bunyips everywhere
And all the locals join the fun
Saying, "Bunyips? Pull the other one!"

"What rubbish! Bunyips don't exist!
You must be going round the twist!"
And sure enough, the tourists flee
For fear they've lost their sanity.

While Murray Bridge is all aglow
With cries of "Thought they'd never go!"
And all along the Murray sands
Are men and bunyips shaking hands.

Doug MacLeod

The Cane Mutiny

Cane toads are obnoxious beasts,
They massacre goannas.
They live in northern Queensland and
They lurk among bernannas.

They're slowly marching from the north
Towards the far horizon;
Their hearts are full of evil and
Their skin is full of pizon.

Attempts to stop this loathesome plague
Are surely doomed to failure;
They'll chomp and kill throughout the land
And toadally wreck Austrailure.

Ann Coleridge

Ravening Horde

Down the mountainside they come,
From the reeking bog.
Tramping through the darkness and
The swirling yellow fog.

Their mud-bespattered hairy legs,
Grotesquely gnarled and scarred,
Stride swiftly through the undergrowth
Although the route is hard.

The hungry gnashing of their teeth
As on their way they go
Strikes terror in the people of
The city down below.

"They're coming," wail the citizens,
"Their food must be prepared;
Kill the fatted calf and see
That no expense is spared.

"We fear the thunder of their tread,
We hear their lusty song,
We dread their endless appetites,
Their eating all day long.

"Heat the water for their baths,
They're cold and they are damp.
Oh horror, they are nearly here—
The Scouts are back from camp."

Ann Coleridge

Attack of the Crayfish From Mars

A spotty young schoolboy called Pontius Gore
Liked films about terror and horror and war
While sensible folk would regard them with
    boredom
The spotty young Ponty would clap and
    applaud 'em.

A film he particularly wanted to see
Was *Attack of the Crayfish from Mars* in 3D
And so, in row L of the Mermaid Palais
Sat Pontius, kicking the heads in row K.

The lights were turned out and the filmshow
    began—
A crash, an explosion, a two-headed man,
A beast with six fingers, a war on the moon
(And they were all just the supporting cartoon).

Then *The Crayfish from Mars*—an abominable
    sight!
With big hairy feelers and eyes burning bright
Some hunters had trapped it but soon it broke
    loose,
It snapped off their legs and it sucked out the juice.

It split them in half with its nuclear ray
Then scooped out their gizzards like people
    mornay,
The audience shuddered, except for brave Pontius
Who made not a sound, since he'd fallen
    unconscious.

Now, night times are different for Pontius Gore
He doesn't go out to the flicks any more,
His mum keeps him home, and you want to know
    how?
The Crayfish from Mars is on video now.

Doug MacLeod

That's the Spirit!

It seems a most rewarding post,
Applying as a trainee ghost
Where one is taught, with moans discreet,
To shake and shimmer in a sheet.
A Mr Dracula's director.
He'll pass you as a spook or spectre.
The discipline is strict, it's true.
You speak when you are spook-en to
Until, come graduation day,
You've frightened everyone away,
A credit to your creepy school.
Well done . . . to every boy and ghoul!

Max Fatchen

Samuel Junior Spook Esquire

Samuel Junior Spook Esquire
Turned up his nose and said,
"No one ever will beat me,
I'll be leader, not led."

"I'll study hard, you wait and see,
I'll study hard and well.
I'll know the witches' alphabet
And every spooky spell."

His friends all cried, "Come play with us,
Put down your fountain pen."
But Samuel answered angrily
"Don't spook to me again!"

"I'll leave you others all behind,
I'll always be ahead.
You'll never be as good as me,
I'll be a super-spook," he said.

Thus Samuel set his friends apart,
He chuckled in his bed.
"They'll never be as good as me,
I'll always be ahead."

While Samuel chuckled heartlessly,
A plan was being formed.
"We'll teach that Samuel Spook Esquire
That friends cannot be scorned."

"Now what has Samuel always wanted?
What's he always said?"
The spooks then nodded, cast the spell,
Now Sam is just a head!

Janeen Brian

The Loof

I'm a Loof—
I'm very independent
and incurious to boot,
insouciant, indifferent:
I couldn't give a hoot.
I don't care what you say of me
in praise or in reproof—
I'm a stolid, apathetic, uninquisitive, ascetic,
    undemonstrative, inscrutable, dispassionate
    and soulless sort of . . .
Loof.

Peter Wesley-Smith

The vampire said: "My name is mud
Because I have a taste for blood
And there are those who think I'm horrid
For nipping victims on the forehead.
But, on this matter I won't hedge.
What really sets my teeth on edge
And scares me even more than rabies
Are children biting jelly babies."

Max Fatchen

You've met your match

Three witches are we, with knobbly toes,
A squint in each eye, a wart on each nose.
We're out to get you, yes we are,
We're searching for you, near and far.

You can't escape, we'll snatch you up,
We've even found an extra cup.
So join us while the coffee bubbles—
We need a fourth for tennis doubles.

Ann Coleridge

Gala Night

Like black and tattered clouds they race
Across the full moon's yellow light,
Squabbling, quibbling, jibbering, jabbering,
Cackling and bickering, blibbing and blabbering,
Crowds of vultures, face to face—
It's the annual witches' gala night!

Above the jagged hills they soar
To where no human ever dares,
Harshlands, marshlands, daggy bog,
Quicksands, blacksands, soggy fog,
The mob descends, all spoiling for
A night of splitting heads and hairs.

The carnival now comes alive
While all the nicer creatures sleep . . .
Broomstick battering, slime bespattering,
Which witch nattering most unflattering,
Wartsnout wins "Nose '85"
And Kark on yardbroom wins the sweep!

Cauldrons spew out frothy juice,
The witches slurp and burp and brawl,
Catfights, batfights, high as flat kites,
Hat frights, hot flights, fang and hate-bites,
Tipsy teams make clever use
Of Hatchet's head as basketball.

The morning shows up mud and leech
And weary witches curse the light,
Too much revelled, too bedevilled,
Too much rivalled, quite dishevelled,
Scratching their goodbyes, they screech
"Let's fight again, next Gala night!"

Stephanie McCarthy

Witches

The moon was red, and overhead
    The witches flew together,
Throughout the night, in silent flight,
    They braved the windy weather.

A single broom within the gloom
    Was gliding at the lead,
But from the rear there came a cheer
    From someone gaining speed.

Then Number Two came flying through
    And overtook the third,
While from the back, along the track,
    Another cheer was heard.

Amid the rush, a scrubbing-brush
    Was gaining second place;
The witch aboard could not afford
    A broom-stick for the race.

While Number One was having fun
    Annoying Number Eight,
A flying mop was forced to stop
    For carrying too much weight.

There came a roar, as Number Four
Was slowly catching up,
But Number Nine had crossed the line
And won the Witches' Cup!

Doug MacLeod

The Curse of Auntie Beth

A family heirloom, handed down
for many generations,
has been the cause of grief untold
and woeful lamentations . . .
Those who own it die a death—
proclaims the curse of Auntie Beth.

My father died at ninety-two,
his dad at ninety-seven;
his dad was eighty-eight years old
when going up to heaven . . .
Those who own it die a death—
proclaims the curse of Auntie Beth.

My great great grandpapa expired
at ninety, drinking whisky;
his pater passed away at four
score years and five, still frisky . . .
Those who own it die a death—
proclaims the curse of Auntie Beth.

And now it's mine, this fatal thing,
this harbinger of sorrow;
the curse will strike me soon, I fear:
I'm ninety-nine tomorrow . . .

Peter Wesley-Smith

Epitaph

I hear a dirge, I see a tomb,
I smell a foetid breath;
I taste the bitter bile of Doom,
I touch the hem of Death:
    Come now, he says, my son,
    come now, your day is done.

A muffled drum, a bell betray
my deepest, darkest fears;
a bugle heralds Judgement Day;
an epitaph appears:
    Here lies, for good or worse,
    the man who wrote this verse.

Peter Wesley-Smith

Epilogue

These terrible poems
Have troubled my head,
I'd better remove it
And go to bed.

Doug MacLeod